# RESOLVING
# CONFLICTS
# ON THE JOB

## The WorkSmart Series

# RESOLVING CONFLICTS ON THE JOB

## Jerry Wisinski

### amacom

## AMERICAN MANAGEMENT ASSOCIATION
## THE WORKSMART SERIES

New York • Atlanta • Boston • Chicago • Kansas City • San Francisco • Washington, D.C.
Brussels • Toronto • Mexico City

This book is available at a special
discount when ordered in bulk quantities.
For information, contact Special Sales Department,
AMACOM, a division of American Management Association,
135 West 50th Street, New York, NY 10020.

This publication is designed to provide accurate and authoritative information in regard to the subject matter covered. It is sold with the understanding that the publisher is not engaged in rendering legal, accounting, or other professional service. If legal advice or other expert assistance is required, the services of a competent professional person should be sought.

Library of Congress Cataloging-in-Publication Data

Wisinski, Jerry.
    Resolving conflicts on the job / Jerry Wisinski.
      p.   cm.
   ISBN 0-8144-7799-2
   1. Conflict management. I. Title.
HD42.W573   1993
650.1'3—dc20           93-9248
                        CIP

Printing number

10  9  8  7  6  5  4  3

To My
Mom and Dad

# CONTENTS

# PREFACE

All relationships, personal and professional, experience some kind of conflict. This is normal, natural, and sometimes even necessary for continued growth and development.

*Resolving Conflicts on the Job* focuses on managing conflict in your professional life. However, many of the techniques described can be applied successfully in managing conflicts in your personal life as well. These techniques include:

- Sources of conflict
- Management methods
- Communication models
- Active listening skills
- Giving and accepting criticism
- Assertiveness theory

Approach and possible outcome varies according to who is involved in the conflict, so there is also a chapter that addresses handling differences with bosses, peers, and employees.

This book is designed to be interractive; in addition to thoroughly examining the elements surrounding conflict, you will find case studies containing questions to answer. In many instances, your current experience will establish the case study itself. Again, there will be questions to help you determine the best approach to dealing with your individual situation.

Some people feel it is best to avoid conflict. While this may be appropriate at times, it is not *always* recommended. The main issue with conflict is not so much that it occurs, but how you manage it when it does. The following chapters will help you examine this concept further and give you the tools you need to manage conflicts when they occur.

# CHAPTER 1

## AN OVERVIEW OF CONFLICT

Conflict. It's a part of our personal lives and a part of our working lives. Although it may not occur on a daily basis, it certainly occurs often enough—for some of us, much too often. But because it is a recurring part of our lives, we need to focus on how best to deal with it rather than pretend it will go away.

## THE POSITIVE VIEW OF CONFLICT

Conflict in the workplace used to be perceived as a negative—something to be avoided at all costs. Associated with undesirable behavior, it was viewed as a characteristic of individuals who couldn't get along with others, weren't team players, or simply didn't fit in. The best way to deal with it was to avoid it.

Today, conflict is viewed much differently. Organizational experts tell us that conflict is normal and natural, and, of course, it is. In addition, it is viewed as an interpersonal dynamic that when handled well can at least be managed, often resolved, and potentially has very creative results. Today, it is critical that we recognize the importance of dealing with conflict rather than adopting the traditional response of avoiding it.

*(Text continues on page 4.)*

# MYTHS AND TRUTHS ABOUT CONFLICT

## Myths

1. *Conflict is dysfunctional in the workplace.* It can be, but it doesn't have to be. When handled effectively, conflict can help ensure successful accomplishment of goals and objectives within your department, perhaps with other departments, and even throughout your entire organization.

2. *Conflict represents communication breakdown.* Quite the contrary. People can interpret the same issue in many different ways. Although conflict can represent an *initial* communication breakdown, it can also provide the opportunity to clarify issues, or reach more creative results.

3. *If avoided, conflict will eventually go away.* Not usually. Minor issues can sometimes resolve themselves, but more often than not, conflicting situations need to be addressed in order for them to be managed.

4. *All conflicts can be resolved.* That would be nice, wouldn't it? However, because you have different values from others, there will be times when you simply can't agree on certain issues. All differences cannot be resolved; however, most can at least be managed.

5. *Conflict always results in a winner and a loser.* Not true. There are many possible outcomes to a conflict. In fact, when mutual desire exists to resolve the differences, you can increase the chances for a "Win/Win" result.

**All differences cannot be resolved; however, most can at least be managed.**

**Truths**

1. *Conflict* will *occur.* Without question. It is a natural dynamic when interacting with others. The more important question is what you do with it when it occurs.

2. *Most conflicts can be managed.* Well, you can't fix everything. But most, if not all, differences can be managed. You have at least five options at your disposal: Competition, Accommodation, Avoidance, Compromise, and Collaboration. Then again, you can always agree to disagree. Most of the time, one of these options will enable you to manage your differences.

3. *Conflict can help build relationships.* This may sound contradictory, but it's true. In attempting to deal with differences that are important to you, it is possible to strengthen relationships with bosses, peers, and employees. Negative first impressions, or bad feelings, may be interpreted differently after further discussion, often resulting in a change in your perception of others and their perception of you.

4. *Conflict can be a motivator for change.* It's certainly possible. In the process of managing your differences, you can become introspective. Through personal examination, you can identify certain behavioral characteristics in your communication skills that can lead to effective change.

**For the 1990s, the ability to manage conflict is a critical interpersonal skill that must be highly developed.**

# WHY DEAL WITH CONFLICT?

For the 1990s, the ability to manage conflict is a critical interpersonal skill that must be highly developed for three major reasons:

1. *To manage change.* Organizations are shifting to a rate faster than ever before. Although some are sizing-up, many are sizing-down. But whatever the direction, change is usually a prelude to many types of conflict.
2. *To understand cultural differences.* As the changing demographics in the workplace move toward the year 2000, your ability to accept, understand, and positively respond to different cultural values will become increasingly more important.
3. *To become effective team members and leaders.* In the past few years, the team concept has experienced a renewed growth. With concepts such as Total Quality Management (TQM), there is a much greater focus on team building. We know conflict will occur in teams, but the end result is the important issue. Was it handled well, or did it hurt the overall team direction?

So why deal with conflict? In short, without the ability to manage conflict, you cannot be successful in your organization. Whatever your position—staff or management, team member or team leader—your ability to effectively manage differences is a critical factor in your personal and professional success.

**Without the ability to manage conflict, you cannot be successful in your organization.**

Please answer the following questions.

1. Who are you currently experiencing differences with at work?

   *Boss(es)/upper management?*

   _____

   _____

_____

_____

_____

*Peers?*

_____

_____

_____

_____

*Employees?*

_____

_____

_____

_____

2. Recently, what conflicts have you handled well?

*Conflict:*

_____

_____

_____

_____

*Result:*

_____

_____

_____

_____

*Conflict:*

_____

_____

_____

_____

_____

*Result:*

_____

_____

_____

_____

_____

3. What conflicts have you *not* handled well?

*Conflict:*

_____

_____

_____

_____

_____

*Result:*

_____

_____

_____

_____

_____

*Conflict:*

_____

_____

_____

_____

_____

*Result:*

_____

_____

_____

_____

_____

4. What do you think the result would be if you confronted the individuals you are currently in conflict with?

   *Name:*

_____

_____

_____

_____

_____

   *Probable result:*

_____

_____

_____

_____

_____

   *Name:*

_____

_____

_____

_____

_____

*Probable result:*

_____

_____

_____

_____

_____

If you found these questions difficult to respond to positively, this book will help give you both an awareness of the issues surrounding conflict in the workplace and the tools to help you manage differences when they occur.

# CHAPTER 2

## SOURCES OF CONFLICT IN THE WORKPLACE

There are two major types of conflict in the workplace: interpersonal and organizational. You would think that of the two, organizational conflict would be the most common. Not so. In fact, most of the differences you are likely to encounter on the job are interpersonally based and perhaps the most difficult to handle.

## INTERPERSONAL CONFLICT

Essentially, interpersonal conflict occurs when you perceive or value a situation differently from the way someone else does. Consider the following case studies.

**Interpersonal conflict occurs when you perceive or value a situation differently from the way someone else does.**

**Case Study 1.** Mary N and her associate Tom are working jointly on a very important project. Currently, the project is on schedule, but just barely. Because they can only work together in the afternoon, Mary suggests staying an hour or so later to gain a little cushion on the deadline. Her associate, however, won't hear of it. The way Tom sees it, he puts in a full day's effort and is not about to give up any personal time. Besides, the project *is* on schedule.

1. What is the potential conflict here?

_____

_____

2. What is Mary's work value regarding the project?

_____

_____

3. What is Tom's work value regarding the project?

_____

_____

Is there a right and wrong in this case study? Or, are there simply two different ways of perceiving the same situation? After all, the project *is* on time.

**Case Study 2.** As a manager, John C. has always performed to the utmost of his ability. He is also a true believer in climbing the corporate ladder.

One of his employees, Peggy, has a great deal of potential for advancing in the organization if she would only apply herself a little more. Peggy's performance is completely acceptable according to company standards, but John C. is convinced she could do better. What's also frustrating to John C. is that Peggy seems to be so involved outside of work. She's president of her son's school PTA and does a lot of volunteer work in her community.

Because of the initiative evidenced by her outside motivation, John C. has tried to explain the potential growth for her in the company, but Peggy just doesn't seem interested.

1. What is the potential conflict here?

_____

_____

2. How does John view success?

_____

_____

3. How might Peggy view success?

_____

_____

4. How do you think John should handle this situation?

_____

_____

It is very easy for us to want others to see things the same way we do—especially about what we would consider to be core work values such as getting a project finished or advancing in our profession. However, we each have our own value system through which we determine our priorities. When these different priorities meet, conflict is usually the result—and how we manage these differences becomes critically important.

## Value Development

**The roots of your value system can be traced back to your early childhood, school years, adolescence, early adulthood, and significant events in your adult life.**

The roots of your value system can be traced back to your early childhood, school years, adolescence, early adulthood, and significant events in your adult life.

But, how are they developed? Why are yours different from others? How do you know which ones are right? Can your values be changed? These are important questions when examining your values in contrast to the values of others.

On page 12 is a chart outlining how value systems are formed. It combines a number of developmental theories and indicates age groupings and major influences within each growth period.

The chart addresses five stages of major influences in a person's development. If your developmental stages were positive, you are likely to have positive expectations for your adult life. On the other hand, if you have been influenced negatively, your expectations are likely to be negative of yourself and others. Although this is not carved in stone, it does constitute a certain amount of probability.

Essentially, your core beliefs are developed throughout the first four stages of growth. As you enter Stage Five (Adulthood-Professional Life), these beliefs become your value system.

# STAGES OF VALUE SYSTEM DEVELOPMENT

**Major Influences**

| | |
|---|---|
| Stage One: Early Childhood<br>Birth to 5 years | *Parents, close relatives, and friends of parents:*<br>Was feedback positive or negative? |
| Stage Two: Early School Years<br>5 years to 10–12 years | *Teachers:*<br>Was feedback positive or negative?<br>*Classmates:*<br>Did you get along with others? Were you made fun of? |
| Stage Three: Teen Years<br>13 years to 17–19 years | *Peer interaction:*<br>Did you fit in? Were you left out? A leader? A follower? Active/not active in organizations, teams? |
| Stage Four: Early Adulthood<br>17–19 years to 21–22 years | *College, military, workplace:*<br>Was feedback the same as in earlier years? Did feedback change with new experiences? Did you question your beliefs about yourself? Did your beliefs change? Remain? |
| Stage Five: Adulthood/ Professional Life | *Spouse, friends, bosses, peers, employees:*<br>Is feedback the same from all groups? Is it positive, negative? Does it vary according to group? Is it different from or the same as in the developmental stages? |

But sometimes these beliefs and expectations are challenged in the workplace by issues unrelated to expertise or job performance. For example, many people were probably raised with the following values or expectations:

*Age:* Younger reports to older.
*Experience:* Less experienced reports to more experienced.
*Sex:* Women report to men.
*Race:* Minorities report to whites.

But what happens when reality reverses these beliefs? Each

reversal of a value expectation opens the possibility for conflict, even though the issue isn't job-related.

Have you ever managed someone who had more experience than you? Had a higher level of education? Was older than you? Were there any conflicts based on these value differences?

_____

_____

_____

Were you ever managed by someone who was less experienced? Had less education? Was younger than you? Were there any conflicts based on these differences?

_____

_____

_____

Are you a woman who has managed men? A minority female who has managed another minority, women or men? A minority female who has managed white men? What could the conflicts be based on these differences?

_____

_____

_____

Are you a man who has been managed by a woman? A minority male who has been managed by a woman of another minority? A white male who has been managed by a minority woman? What could the conflicts be based on these differences?

_____

_____

_____

With these elements in mind, consider the following case study.

**Case Study.** Holly T. is a black woman, age 31. She has a bachelor's degree in mechanical engineering and six years of work experience. Recently she was hired by XYZ Engineering to manage a department of three employees. Her staff consists of two men and one woman.

Mel L.:     Black male; age 45; BS, Engineering; twenty-three years' experience; two years with XYZ.

Mike D.:    White male; age 33; BS, Engineering; ten years' experience; seven years with XYZ.

Maria Z.:   Mexican-American female; age 26; BS, Engineering; five years experience, all with XYZ.

What are the potential conflicts with each employee in this case study?

**Mel L.:**

_____

_____

_____


**Mike D.:**

_____

_____

_____


**Maria Z.:**

_____

_____

_____

The potential for conflict among these people is great. The point is, these probable conflicts are interpersonally rather than organizationally based. They are rooted in an individual's value system rather than in an individual's ability to perform the job. We often automatically make certain negative assumptions based on a person's profile rather than his or her job performance.

## Can Value Systems Be Changed?

Your core values cannot be erased; that is, you can't change what you've been taught. But you can learn new perspectives and ways of modifying your behavior.

By initially identifying and admitting your personal feelings, then adopting a wait-and-see attitude, you decrease the potential for conflict based solely on someone's profile. You also open yourself to further personal development and wider perspectives regarding other people's abilities.

# ORGANIZATIONAL CONFLICT

**Organizational conflict is a by-product of changing dynamics within a structure.**

Organizational conflict is not based on personal value systems; it is a by-product of changing dynamics within a structure. When left unattended, these dynamics cause conflict within the organization. If these forces clash with personal values, then interpersonal conflict can also occur.

### Sources of Organizational Conflict

1. *Change.* Some change within an organization is normal, and to be expected. New policies, changes in operational procedures, and a certain amount of employee turnover are common internal changes all organizations experience. Externally, municipal, state, or federal legislation can also require an organization to make specific changes. But other forms of change are more drastic. Reorganizations and "right-sizing" (gobbledegook for layoffs) can wreak havoc in organizations, threatening the job security of everyone. Even growth can cause conflict. Although growth is normally seen as good for an organization, communication breakdown is sure to occur, responsibilities change, and reporting relationships may be shuffled. Change within an organization definitely causes conflict.

2. *Conflicting goals and objectives.* Usually this is the result of poor communication and planning. The goals and objectives of one department may clash with those of another department. Better communication between department heads can usually resolve the issue.

3. *Limited resources.* Limited resources can mean practically anything: not enough employees, lack of space, shortage of finances, outdated equipment, and so on. These and similar problems can cause organizational conflict by limiting expected performance of individuals, departments, and perhaps even the organization as a whole.

4. *The domino effect.* The domino effect is the product of poor planning and communication breakdown. It occurs when the activities of one department have a direct impact on the activities of another department, the activities of which have a direct impact on another department, and on and on.

**The domino effect is the product of poor planning and communication breakdown.**

**Example:** The director of sales has promised his employees an all-expenses-paid trip to Hawaii if they increase widget sales by 15 percent over the next quarter. The sales staff is really excited, and sales begin increasing immediately. However, no one has told the production department, which immediately falls behind; or the shipping department, which won't have enough widget boxes if production catches up; or customer service, which will surely become involved when the widgets don't arrive as promised by the salespeople who wanted to go to Hawaii. In this example, it is the responsibility of the director of sales to inform other department heads of the proposed change so they can make the necessary adjustments in advance of rather than after the fact.

Because organizational conflict can easily cause additional interpersonal differences, it is the responsibility of upper management, department heads, and supervisors to minimize the effects of these sources through responsible communication with each other and with their employees.

# CHAPTER 3

## FIVE METHODS FOR MANAGING CONFLICT

As stated in Chapter 1, conflict is inevitable. But the real issue is how we deal with it. We can't always avoid it, nor can we always resolve it, but we can usually manage it to some conclusion. Following are five methods of managing conflict and some appropriate uses for each.

### COMPETITION (WIN/LOSE)

**The Competition approach to conflict is an attempt at complete dominance.**

The Competition approach to conflict is an attempt at complete dominance. It is a "winner takes all" position. Usually, the focus is on winning the conflict at all costs, rather than searching for the most appropriate solution for everyone involved.

Win/Lose is a power-based mode. You use whatever power you think you have available to win people over to your position. Ability to argue, rank in the organization, economic sanctions, coercion, and force are common strategies used with the Competition approach to conflict.

These characteristics may lead you to believe that Competition would rarely be useful in the workplace. However, there are times when the Win/Lose approach is appropriate.

*Appropriate Uses of the Competition Approach*

- In emergencies when quick, decisive action is needed
- In situations where unpopular changes need to be implemented

17

- When other methods have been tried and failed
- In working relationships where there is an atmosphere of low trust

## ACCOMMODATION (LOSE/WIN)

Accommodation is the opposite of the Competition approach. With this method, you are willing to yield your position to the other person. Although this may appear to be a nonassertive behavior, it really isn't. However, Nonassertives often adopt the Accommodation method as their only method of coping with conflict. But this is an inappropriate application of the Accommodation approach, implying an unwillingness to attempt to resolve the differences, and a preference for avoidance in the face of a potentially unpleasant situation.

**You can actually assertively choose to be nonassertive.**

Effective application of the Lose/Win approach comes from an assertive position. You can actually assertively choose to be nonassertive for reasons other than timidity or avoidance.

### Appropriate Uses of Accommodation

- When it is more important to preserve the relationship than argue the issue
- When the issue is more important to the other person than it is to you
- When you want to indicate a degree of reasonableness
- When you want to encourage others to express their own point of view
- When you want others to learn by their own choices and actions

## AVOIDANCE (LOSE/LOSE)

On the surface, the Avoidance approach appears to be inappropriate for resolving differences. When nonassertively applied, it indicates an unwillingness to cooperate, denial that a problem exists, or withdrawal from a threatening situation. When you use Avoidance in this manner, you forfeit personal gain as well as any potential contribution to the working relationship. It is referred to as the Lose/Lose outcome, because neither party is able to even deal with the issue, much less manage or resolve it.

**When appropriately applied, avoidance can actually help resolve differences between two people.**

However, when appropriately applied, Avoidance can actually help resolve differences between two people.

**Example:** In the heat of an argument when nothing seems to be getting accomplished, temporary Avoidance or diffusion gives each party time to cool off: "Phil, this isn't getting us anywhere. Why don't we give it a rest for a while and discuss it later when we've both calmed down a little, OK?"

When this approach is used, it is important that the person who calls the "time out" initiate the issue again within an appropriate amount of time. If this doesn't happen, the temporary diffusion can be perceived as a manipulative move used to simply ignore or avoid the issue entirely.

### Appropriate Uses of Avoidance

- If others can resolve the conflict more effectively
- If both parties see the issue to be a minor one
- If the negative impact of the situation itself may be too damaging or costly to both parties involved
- If additional time is required
- If both parties need a chance to cool off

## COMPROMISE (WIN/LOSE–WIN/LOSE)

The Compromise approach to conflict resolution involves negotiation, tradeoffs, swapping, and a high degree of flexibility. It is referred to as the Win/Lose–Win/Lose position because, though you will get some of what you want, you will also have to give up something else in the process.

It is important to decide in advance how much you are willing to give away before you begin to negotiate. In other words, you need to set limits. But this doesn't necessarily mean you will have to give away everything up to that point; setting limits in advance simply gives you a range within which you can negotiate effectively.

When using Compromise to resolve differences, you indicate concern not only for your own objectives but also maintenance of the relationship. Compromise is an attempt to find the common ground of agreement. Both parties win some aspects of the issue while giving up others.

### *Appropriate Uses of Compromise:*

- To reach agreement when both sides have equal power
- To find a common ground when both parties have competing goals
- To achieve temporary settlement in complex matters
- To reach a solution under difficult circumstances or time pressures
- To maintain personal objectives while preserving the relationship

## COLLABORATION (WIN/WIN)

Collaboration is usually considered the best, but the most difficult, method of managing differences between two people. When using Collaboration to resolve conflict, there is a maximum concern for the issues and for the maintenance of the relationship on both sides. It is both an Assertive and Collaborative approach.

Collaboration also attempts to establish a climate that will enable each person to examine and understand the other person's point of view. It is referred to as Win/Win because it involves identifying those areas where agreements exist and where there are differences, evaluating alternatives, and selecting solutions that have the full support and commitment of both parties.

This kind of problem solving requires an atmosphere of trust, the surfacing of hidden agendas, and the willingness to be creative in order to reach resolution. Additionally, certain conditions must be agreed to in order to achieve the Win/Win result.

### Conditions for Successful Collaboration

> **Agreement isn't the issue. The point is to accept, under- stand, and validate the other person's feelings.**

- *Willingness to resolve.* Both parties *must* be willing to resolve the conflict. Any hidden agendas or failure to trust or to be honest will not result in the Win/Win result.
- *Willingness to go to the root problem.* Often, what appears to be the problem is only a symptom of the real issue. Both parties must be willing to explore the origins of the conflict in order to identify its true source and deal with it.
- *Willingness to empathize.* Feelings are always a part of conflict. Both sides need to be willing to accept and understand the other person's feelings and point of view, even though they might not agree with each other. Agreement isn't the issue. The point is to accept, understand, and validate the other person's feelings.

### Appropriate Uses of Collaboration

- For preserving important objectives that can't be compromised while still maintaining the relationship
- For merging experiences and feelings from people who have different backgrounds and perspectives
- For indicating creativeness by being willing to explore alternatives together that neither party might have thought of individually
- To get at unresolved root problems that may have hindered the working relationship over a long period of time

Differences will occur between individuals. We know that. Choosing the most appropriate management method according to the situation is the key to handling one of the most common dynamics in human interaction in the workplace.

# CHAPTER 4

## COMMUNICATION MODELS FOR RESOLVING DIFFERENCES

In addition to the five methods of managing conflict, it might also be helpful to consider some communication models that can be used in conjunction with them.

### THE SIX-STEP MODEL

**The more both parties are able to go through the steps together, the greater is the possibility of a successful conclusion.**

The Six-Step Model for resolving differences is particularly helpful in identifying and managing organizational conflict. It can also be applied in situations between managers and employees. The more both parties are able to go through the steps together, the greater is the possibility of a successful conclusion.

In addition, this model not only helps with whatever the current problem might be, but establishes a format for dealing with future situations.

*Six Steps to Resolving Differences*

1. *Define the apparent conflict.* Initially defining what you think the problem is is critical to finding a solution. It is not only important for you to state what *you* think the problem is; it is also important to speculate how the *other party* might see the conflict. By employing this first step, you establish an orientation toward resolving the differences.

2. *Analyze the situation.* After you've stated what you think the problem is, it is helpful to ask the following critical questions in order to further analyze the situation.

- *Who?* Who is involved? It's important that all parties involved in the conflict are identified.
- *What?* What exactly has happened? What were the circumstances?
- *Where?* Where did the conflict occur? Could the place be significant?
- *When?* When did this occur? Has it been going on for a while? If so, why wasn't it dealt with in a timely fashion? Is it too late to address the issue? Is it a recent occurrence? Is this the appropriate time to address the issue?
- *Why?* Why did the conflict occur? Is it significant that these were the individuals involved? Could it have been prevented? Should it have been?
- *How?* How did the conflict occur? What happened that shouldn't have? What wasn't happening that should have been?

**By analyz-
ing the
situation,
it is possi-
ble to dis-
cover that
what you
thought
was the
original
problem in
fact isn't.**

By analyzing the situation, it is possible to discover that what you thought was the original problem in fact isn't. If this becomes apparent after the analysis, you simply redefine the conflict based on your new information.

3. *Generate alternatives.* There are many ways to solve a given situation. When attempting to manage differences, you need to generate a number of possible options. To avoid setting precedence or possible legal problems, it is also helpful to consider some basic organizational questions in determining your approach to the problem.

- Has this situation happened before? If so, what was done about it?
- Is there an existing policy or procedure that would help determine the solution?
- How will similar situations in the future be affected by the solution? Will a precedent be established?

4. *Project the results of each alternative.* By projecting the results of each possible choice, you help ensure the success of your efforts. By selecting each alternative and asking the question, "What if . . . ?" you can potentially project the end result of your selection.

5. *Select and agree on the alternative.* After examining your options and potential outcomes, the next step is to select the most appropriate option. Although success is never guaranteed, you should feel confident at this point that you have arrived at the best solution for everyone involved, given the information at your disposal.

6. *Implement and evaluate.* When implementing your solution, you need to determine its success or failure through evaluation. This is accomplished best by agreeing to follow-up dates where the parties involved meet to determine the degree of success of the solution. Both the frequency and the length of the evaluation process should be determined by the importance of the original issue.

What organizational conflicts are you currently experiencing that this Six-Step Method could be applied to?

1. _____

  _____

2. _____

  _____

3. _____

  _____

In addition to the general Six-Step Method, there are two other excellent models that can be used to help settle differences.

## The DESC Model

The DESC Model is a rather direct method for dealing with conflict between two people. It is sometimes perceived as being competitive and often results in a Win/Lose outcome, but it can be very effective when other methods have not succeeded. Although it can be used when relating to bosses or peers, it is most often used by supervisors and managers dealing with uncooperative employees. The steps for the DESC Model are as follows:

• **D**—*Describe the situation.* It is important to be very specific in this first step. Describe the differences or the other person's behavior as clearly as possible. Use specific incidents wherever possible as this helps prevent general statements.

• **E**—*Express your feelings.* If the individual isn't aware that his or her actions are having a negative impact on you or others, there's no reason for the individual to think there is a problem in the first place. Expressing your feelings lets the individual know clearly that the problem is not acceptable and must be resolved.

• **S**—*Specify what you want to happen.* After you've indicated your response to the situation, you then indicate the changes you expect in the other person. Here again, be specific so there is little chance for misinterpretation. Included in this step is, What's In It For Them? (WIIFT?). You can't expect others to do something just because you want them to; you need to sell them on the idea. People respond much more positively when they can buy into the reason for changing their actions or behavior.

• **C**—*Consequences.* The final step in the DESC Model is to let the other person know the expected result. It is probably best to indicate the possible negative consequences first, but it is critical that you are both willing and able to follow through with this alternative if changes are not made. The last part of this step is to emphasize the potentially positive results to be realized if the requested changes are made.

> You can't expect others to do something just because you want them to; you need to sell them on the idea.

**Example of the DESC Model.** Brigette B. is an office manager in a consulting firm. Although she usually consults with her employees on many situations, like all managers she must make certain decisions on her own and then inform her employees. She then expects them to follow her directions.

Recently, she has been experiencing difficulty with one of her more experienced employees. Ed offers a lot of suggestions when consulted, but he openly disagrees with Brigette when she makes a decision on her own; then he refuses to follow her directions. She has discussed this with him on two occasions, but it hasn't helped. She has called him in for a third meeting on the same issue and has decided to use the DESC Model.

### Describe
"Ed, in the past week you have openly disagreed with me on two decisions I've made concerning procedures here in the office. More importantly, you haven't followed my directions regarding those decisions." [*She lists the decisions and disagreements*].

### Express
"I am frustrated and angry at this point because we've had this discussion twice before." [*She states explicitly when the previous discussions occurred.*]

### Specify
"Although you may have the right to disagree with decisions I make without your consultation, I still expect you to comply with them and do what I ask you to do. It hurts the team effort when one member refuses to cooperate. On the other hand, it makes the job easier on everyone when you pitch in and do your share." [*WIIFT?*]

### Consequence
[*Negative*]: "Ed, I expect we won't have to have this conversation again. If we do, I'll consider it a formal disciplinary step."

[*Positive*]: "On the other hand, I want to be able to work this out. When I do confer with you and the other employees, I get excellent feedback, and I want that to continue."

The DESC Model is better suited to dealing with situations that have become serious. It is also useful when one party needs to exercise a certain amount of control over another. Therefore, we need to choose the occasion to use this method carefully.

To increase the effectiveness of this method, advance preparation is a must. This means outlining your basic thoughts in advance.

Is there a situation where the DESC Model would be helpful? If so, use the following form to outline your approach.

1.  Describe the situation (briefly).

    _____

    _____

2.  Express your feelings.

    _____

    _____

3.  Specify what you want to happen.

    _____

    _____

4.  Determine the consequences. What will happen if the other party doesn't comply? Does comply?

    _____

    _____

    _____

**Positive Intentionality assumes the other person means well, and is not tryng to cause a conflict.**

# THE AEIOU MODEL

The AEIOU Model for managing differences is effective with any level within the organization: employee to boss, peer to peer, or boss to employee. Focusing on Collaboration, or the Win/Win outcome, the key to this approach is a concept known as *Positive Intentionality* (sounds complex, but it's really simple).

Positive Intentionality assumes the other person means well and is not trying to cause a conflict.

**Example.** Your boss delegates important projects to you because you have a strong background and are well-experienced. However, after the project has been delegated, your boss constantly checks with you "just to see how it's going." You find this aggravating and you're beginning to feel that you're not trusted.

If you approach your boss to discuss this and begin with a question such as, "Why are you constantly looking over my shoulder when you assign me to a project?" you'll come across as accusatory, automatically putting your boss on the defense.

With Positive Intentionality, you attempt to identify a positive reason in your boss's mind for his or her action.

Perhaps your boss simply wants to make sure everything is going right; therefore, the intention of the double-checking is positive, and does not indicate distrust.

After you've identified a positive intention, you can then use it to open the issue without putting your boss on the defensive. For example, if you say, "I know you're concerned about completing those projects we were given at the last minute," you are identifying with your boss's concern rather than accusing his/her action.

Following are the steps in the AEIOU Model.

- **A**—*Assume the other person means well.* If you assume the other person is trying to cause conflict, the chances for effectively managing the situation are greatly reduced. However, if you attempt to identify a positive intention and state it to the other person, you substantially increase the possibility of resolving the differences.

- **E**—*Express your feelings.* After you've indicated to the person what you perceive to be a positive intention, you then respond by affirming that position and expressing your own specific concern.

- **I**—*Identify what you would like to happen.* In this step, you nondefensively propose the changes you would like to

**Although you need to be firm in your approach, the language you choose is very important.**

see occur. Although you need to be firm in your approach, the language you choose is very important. Saying "I want . . ." is extremely different from saying "I would like. . . ." The former may cause defensiveness; the latter is nonthreatening.

• **O**—*Outcome expected.* As in the DESC Model, there are both negative and positive outcomes possible. Although it is important to indicate the potential negative outcome, it is most important to emphasize the positive expectations for both of you (WIIFT?)

• **U**—*Understanding on a mutual basis.* In this final stage of the AEIOU Model, the aim is to get the other person to agree to your proposal. A good way to do this is to ask, "Could we agree to this for a while and see if it works out for both of us?" Of course, there are always two sides to the story, so you need to be ready to consider Compromise or alternative options in this step.

**Example of the AEIOU Model:** Following is an application of the AEIOU Model using the example of the overly concerned boss.

**Assume**
"Al, I know you're concerned about finishing those projects that were dumped on us last week."

**Express**
"I'm also concerned about getting them finished and I'm willing to do whatever it takes to get them done. I'm also a little concerned about our working relationship, and I'd like to talk to you about it. Do you have a minute?"

**Identify**
"When you delegate a project, it seems like you're continually checking up on me. I know you've said you just want to see how it's going but it bothers me, and I'm beginning to feel you don't trust me.

"What I would like is for us to agree to certain dates where we can review my progress. If I run into any problems I can't handle before we get together, I'll be sure to come and see you."

### Outcome

"Al, if things continue as they have been, I'll become increasingly concerned about your trust in me, and I really want to avoid that. But if we can agree to what I'm asking, I'll feel better about the delegation, and you can rest assured that the job is getting done."

### Understanding

"Could we try this for a while to see if it will work for both of us? What do you think?"

Is there a situation you are currently in that would lead itself to the AEIOU Model? Use the following form to outline your thoughts.

## The AEIOU Model

1. Assume the other person means well (identify possible Positive Intention).

   _____

   _____


2. Express your feelings (verify Positive Intention and state your concerns).

   _____


3. Identify what you would like to happen.

   _____

   _____


4. Project the Outcome. What will the negative results be? What will the positive results be?

   _____

_____

_____

5. Define the Understanding. What can both parties agree to?

_____

_____

**You must be aware that very few things ever go exactly as you think they will.**

Whatever model you choose (Six-Step, DESC, AEIOU), you must be aware that very few things ever go exactly as you think they will. Preparing in advance and a willingness to be flexible when possible will help you manage differences with others. Following are some guidelines for planning your approach.

### Guidelines for Planning Your Approach

1. Anticipate the other person's reactions. How is he or she likely to respond to each step?
2. Where do you think the greatest point of resistance will be? What can you do to overcome it without causing greater conflict?
3. When is the best time to approach this person?
4. Be sure to establish "What's In It For Them?" (WIIFT?) when preparing your approach.
5. Outline the key phrases in your model. Don't write paragraphs or even sentences—one or two phrases for each step is enough. Bring these notes with you to be sure all steps are covered and you're not thrown off track.

In choosing any of these approaches, it is important that you consider both the situation and the individual(s) involved. Although each method is valid, choosing the most appropriate model will help ensure your success in attempting to resolve whatever differences you may encounter.

# CHAPTER 5

## USING ACTIVE LISTENING AND RESPONDING SKILLS FOR RESOLVING DIFFERENCES

Most of us think we're good listeners. Most of us aren't.

Listening is not the natural process we think it is because of the time difference between the relatively slow rate of speech compared to the much faster rate of processing. On the average, we speak at approximately 125–150 wpm, depending on the part of the country we were raised in and where we currently live. For example, if we're from the Northeast, we talk "very fast"; if we're from the South, we talk "rather slow." However, no matter where we're from, our processing rate is four to six times our speaking rate. In short, we can process much faster than someone else can talk.

This leaves us with a lot of free time to do other things while the other person is speaking. We drift off, fantasize, or travel down our mind's highway, on a mental vacation. Of course, every now and then we check back in by nodding our head, muttering "uh-huh," or "oh really," or "no kidding?" or whatever. But we're not really *listening*, and we're certainly not responding.

## FIVE LEVELS OF ACTIVE LISTENING AND RESPONDING SKILLS

Following is a listing of five levels of active listening and responding skills. They begin with the simple and graduate to the more complex.

## Level 1. Basic Acknowledgments

Some of the basic acknowledgments have already been mentioned. Nonverbal responses include head-nodding, leaning forward or backward, folding or unfolding arms, making eye contact or looking away, and so on. Verbal responses include "uh-huh," "oh really?" "no kidding?" "nah," "huh?" and so on.

Although these responses are basic, they are nonetheless necessary in letting the speaker know you're listening. Of course, you can use these same responses to take that mental vacation discussed earlier. But the positive intention of these basic acknowledgments is to indicate you are actively listening to what's being said.

## Level 2. Silence

As the saying goes, "Silence is golden." This statement could not be truer than when applied to managing conflict. However, silence is difficult for most of us. We are conditioned to speak rather than listen. But when we are able to discipline ourselves to be silent, we usually find out more information from the speaker.

When you reach a natural pause in what you're saying, you normally expect the listener to respond to you. If there is silence, you probably will have a tendency to add additional information. A good interviewer uses this method when trying to get at information the interviewee may not have originally wanted to reveal.

## Level 3. Questions

**How can you be listening if you're asking questions?**

The idea of asking questions may seem contradictory at first: How can you be listening if you're asking questions? In fact, asking questions not only tells the speaker you're interested in what is being said, it also tells the speaker you want to know more. Asking questions helps to gain a better understanding of the other person's point of view.

## Level 4. Paraphrasing

Paraphrasing is a response tool used to verify understanding on the part of the listener. It focuses on content, and involves interpreting what you think the speaker said, then getting verification that you are correct. There are certain steps to take when using the paraphrasing process. They are outlined in the box below.

**A courteous interruption is sometimes appropriate.**

## STEPS FOR PARAPHRASING

1. *Let the other person finish speaking.* Although this is generally the rule, a courteous interruption is sometimes appropriate. Beginning with a phrase such as, "Excuse me, but let me see if I understand what you're saying," is better than not interrupting and then misunderstanding the message.

2. *Restate what you think the other person has said.* The intent here is not to parrot the speaker, but to repeat in your own words what you think has been said.

3. *If the speaker confirms your understanding, continue the conversation.*

4. *If the speaker indicates you misunderstood, ask the speaker to repeat.* When attempting to resolve differences, how you handle your misunderstandings is important. If you tell someone, "You're not making yourself clear . . .", you may sound accusatory and perhaps intensify the situation. Conversely, if you say, "I'm not understanding you; could you say that again?" you are remaining neutral while asking for clarification.

There is one caution when using paraphrasing: Don't over-use it. You can always tell when someone has just completed a course in listening skills. After passing them in the hallway, you nod and say, "Good mornin', how ya' doin'?" If they stop you and say, "Excuse me, let me see if I understand what you're saying . . .", they've just been to a seminar and are in the midst of paraphrasing everything.

Paraphrasing should be used for three main reasons:

1. To summarize
2. To clarify a critical thought
3. To confirm your understanding

It is not intended to be used in superficial conversations.

## Level 5. Reflective Listening

**If you are emotionally involved, it is very easy to sound accusatory rather than concerned.**

As was stated before, paraphrasing focuses on clarity of content. In contrast, reflective listening focuses on responding to the speaker's emotion.

Reflective listening is considered to be a very high level of response because the listener identifies and responds to the speaker's apparent emotion by filtering through the content. Although counselors and therapists typically use this technique, it requires a lot of practice to master. How you phrase your statements is critical. If you are emotionally involved, it is very easy to sound accusatory rather than concerned.

The real value of reflective listening is that it truly tells the speaker you are listening. When you combine it with paraphrasing, you are using the most sophisticated of all the listening skills.

1. Who is the best listener you know?

_____

2. What specifically does this person do when listening?

_____

---

## EXAMPLES OF REFLECTIVE LISTENING

### Accusatory Reflective Statements

"Well, look at this, you're ___(emotion)___ ."

"Go ahead, feel ___(emotion)___ ."

"I knew you would react like a(an)
___(emotion)___ person."

### Concerned Reflective Statements

"You seem ___(emotion)___ about this."

"I'm concerned about your ___(emotion )___ ."

"I think you're feeling ___(emotion)___ right
now."

---

**Most excessive talkers don't realize they talk too much—probably because no one's ever told them. Even if they were told, they probably weren't listening.**

3. How are you *perceived* as a listener? What levels do you currently use? Which do you need to develop?

## LISTENING AND RESPONDING TO THE EXCESSIVE TALKER

Most excessive talkers don't realize they talk too much—probably because no one's ever told them. Even if they were told, they probably weren't listening.

Some people feel the need to give us all the details before getting to their point. To them, *everything* is important. Others want you to realize how hard they worked to get something done. Then it seems there are those who talk just to hear their own voice.

Listening and responding to the excessive talker is difficult, but not impossible. However, you must control the conversation in order to get the information you need. There are two tools you can use to do this.

1. *Interrupting*. As a child, you were probably taught not to interrupt, but you can use interrupting to control the speaker. Phrases such as "Excuse me, but . . ." or "Let me see if I understand you . . ." allow us to break into the conversation and ask for specific information without putting the speaker on the defensive.
2. *Focusing*. In effect, focusing is asking the speaker to come to the point. A simple phrase such as, "So your point is . . ." or "Then the bottom line is . . .", will usually help put the conversation back on track.

For these two tools to be effective, however, you must use them repeatedly. Hopefully, the speaker will eventually get to the point.

Although these tools help you to control a conversation, they don't deal with the real issue. Depending on your relationship with the speaker, perhaps you could use the DESC or the AEIOU models to let the speaker know that his or her excessive talking is not appropriate. We run the risk of hurting feelings or perhaps causing temporary conflict, but it may help in the long run, making it worth the effort.

When attempting to manage conflict, practicing developed listening and responding skills is an absolute must. How you listen tells others how you are receiving them. You simply cannot resolve differences effectively if you aren't willing to actively listen and respond to others appropriately.

# CHAPTER 6

## CRITICISM AND CONFLICT

Very few of us like to be criticized—or like to formally criticize others, for that matter. But in the workplace we are sometimes called on to criticize an employee for poor performance or inappropriate behavior, or a peer for not pulling his or her weight, or perhaps even our boss in certain situations (though this is not usually recommended).

Criticism can cause differences between people, but if handled correctly, you can reduce the probability of the criticism resulting in conflict. And if you are on the receiving end, if you accept the criticism nondefensively, the probability of conflict is again minimized.

**Generally, there are two types of criticism. Constructive criticism focuses on positive intention. Destructive criticism focuses on negative put downs.**

## Types of Criticism

Generally, there are two types of criticism. Constructive criticism focuses on positive intention. Destructive criticism focuses on negative put downs.

### Constructive Criticism

Constructive criticism is positively intentioned and in the work setting, usually applies to performance that needs improvement or behavior that needs to be changed in some way. In constructive criticism, the focus is on the issue, not on the person. Although you're asking for a change, you're not attacking the individual.

A good example of this might be the annual performance appraisal—that we all love so much. Here, the intention is to discuss both performance and behavior and indicate where, if necessary, each could be improved. However, the performance appraisal is a regularly scheduled event in the workplace. But there are times that are not expected when you still may have to give criticism to someone. These situations must be handled very carefully to get the positive result you want and not cause further conflict. Consider the questions in the box on page 40 when determining when and how to use constructive criticism.

Is there someone you need to criticize constructively? If so, answer the following questions to help you prepare your approach.

**These situations must be handled very carefully to get the positive result you want and not cause further conflict.**

1. Is the issue performance- or behavior-based?

   _____

2. If it is performance-based, are company standards being met? If company standards are not being met, where specifically is improvement needed?

   _____

   _____

   _____

3. If it is behavior-based, what specifically happened? What changes need to be made?

   _____

   _____

   _____

4. What specific suggestions do you have?

   _____

   _____

   _____

5. When is the best time to approach this individual?

_____

_____

Giving crit-
icism is
sensitive
at best.
You need to
be sure
you've
selected
the right
time and
place to
address
the individ-
ual.

## QUESTIONS FOR USING CONSTRUCTIVE CRITICISM

1. _Is the issue performance- or behavior-based?_ This question helps you determine your approach to the situation.
2. _If it is performance-based, are the company standards being met?_ If company standards are being met, you may have an interpersonal value difference, not a performance problem. If company standards are not being met, where specifically is improvement needed?
3. _If it is behavior-based, what specifically happened? What changes need to be made?_ When discussing behavior as an issue, it is critical that you be as specific as possible with dates, times, and a clear description of the behavior that occurred and the changes that are expected.
4. _Are you ready with specific suggestions for the individual?_ Constructive criticism involves two parts: making the criticism, and then offering helpful suggestions for improvement.
5. _Is the timing right? When should you approach the individual?_ Giving constructive criticism is sensitive at best. You need to be sure you've selected the right time and place to address the individual.

## Destructive Criticism

While constructive criticism can be used to reduce differences, destructive criticism provokes differences and intentionally causes conflict.

Destructive criticism attacks the person rather than dealing with issues of performance or behavior. It is an aggressive attempt to put down or dominate the other person. Oddly enough, although the outcome of this form of criticism is always negative, it isn't always negatively intended. We are all capable of negative criticism when we are angry at someone. Perhaps this is an example of the timing not being right to deal with that individual.

In the box on page 42 are some ways to avoid giving destructive criticism.

**Being able to accept the way others see you shows maturity on your part and enables you to make changes where necessary.**

# RECEIVING CRITICISM

To be effective in managing conflict, it is important that you not only know how to *give* criticism, but also how to *accept* it from others, even when you perceive their intent as being destructive. Being able to accept the way others see you shows maturity on your part and enables you to make changes where necessary.

# CONSIDERATIONS FOR ACCEPTING CRITICISM

1. *Is the criticism accurate?* If the criticism is valid, you need to be able to accept it and admit it in a nondefensive manner. This is often referred to as Negative Assertion.

• **Negative Assertion**

Negative Assertion is a nondefensive response used to confirm the criticism leveled at you. By agreeing with

# WAYS TO AVOID GIVING DESTRUCTIVE CRITICISM

1. *Don't deal with the situation when you're angry.* The temptation is too great to attack the person rather than the issue.
2. *Focus on the issue or behavior, not the personality.* This increases the chances for resolving the differences; if you focus on the personality, you only deepen the conflict.
3. *Use neutral language rather than beginning sentences with "you".* Using phrases such as "This problem . . ." or "This behavior . . ." will help toward resolution. Using openings such as "You're always . . ." or "You never . . ." are accusatory and place the other person on the defensive.
4. *Indicate your desire to resolve the difference.* This helps to establish a nondefensive atmosphere where negotions can occur.
5. *Use the DESC or the AEIOU Models.* These models are specifically designed to avoid defensiveness when giving constructive criticism.

the criticism when it could be true, you usually prevent the conflict from escalating any further.

## Example

*Criticism:*

"You're constantly expecting me to do more than everyone else. I don't think that's very fair."

*Negative Assertion:*

"You're probably right. I can understand why you might feel that way even though that isn't my intent."

When using Negative Assertion, you open up the possibility for further discussion without being defensive while admitting the possible truth of the criticism.

2. *Is the criticism questionable?* If you don't understand the criticism you can still avoid responding defensively by using a method known as Negative Inquiry.

- **Negative Inquiry**

  Negative Inquiry allows you to question the criticism for more specific information. As you question the other person you can assess the feelings expressed to you and also determine if the criticism is accurate.

**Example:**

*Criticism:*

"You need to start doing a better job in the future."

*Response:*

"Is there something wrong with my work?"

*Criticism:*

"Yes there is—it just isn't up to par."

*Response:*

"Could you be more specific?"

*Criticism:*

"Sure I can. For example, you barely finished the last two assignments on time, and there were too many errors."

*Response:*

"You're right (*Negative Assertion*), I did have a tough time getting those assignments done, but I wasn't aware of the errors. Can you tell me what they were?" [*They discuss the errors.*]

*Response:*

"Is there anything else?"

*Criticism:*

"No, not really—I'm just concerned about you staying on schedule and not making so many mistakes."

*Response:*

"I appreciate your feedback. I'll try to be more aware of my time, and more careful about my work. Please let me know if you see an improvement."

Although this example might seem a little unreal, consider the alternative. The boss criticizes the employee, the employee becomes defensive, and there are angry feelings with no resolution.

**Sometimes people like to criticize for the sake of starting a conflict.**

There is a secondary aspect to using either Negative Assertion or Negative Inquiry. Sometimes people like to criticize for the sake of starting a conflict. In the case of Negative Assertion, agreeing with the criticism (when it's accurate) usually stops the accusation midstream. In the case of Negative Inquiry, asking for specifics throws the ball back into the accusor's court. If the accusor doesn't have specifics, it takes away momentum. If the accusor does have specifics, you have the opportunity to indicate your willingness to accept the criticism and make changes where necessary.

## HANDLING OTHER PEOPLE'S ANGER

Knowing how to handle other people's anger is an important quality in dealing with conflict in the workplace. Destructive criticism is often accompanied by anger, and it is nearly impossible to settle differences when emotions are in the way. However, there is a two-step method for dealing with this type of situation.

### The Two-Step Method for Dealing With Anger

1. *Allow the person to release the emotion.* As mentioned, it is nearly impossible to resolve the issue when emotions are in the way. So, your first step is to allow the person to rid him- or herself of emotion. It is *very* important not to take things personally when attempting this first step. If that happens, there are two people dumping on each other, getting nowhere fast.

Using statements like, "I can see you're upset," or "I can understand why you're angry," should help in this step. Although these statements indicate empathy, they do not necessarily indicate agreement. However, at no time should you allow someone to be verbally abusive toward you. Such behavior is totally inappropriate and should never be tolerated.

2. *Deal with the content.* After the individual has released his or her anger, you can then begin to explore the reasons for that feeling. This is a perfect time to use Negative Inquiry to get to the source and then Negative Assertion where appropriate. After the real situation is revealed, both parties have the opportunity to resolve or at least manage the conflict.

**After the real situation is revealed, both parties have the opportunity to resolve or at least manage the conflict.**

These two steps for handling other people's anger come from basic customer service. In one well-documented case, a customer had bought a rather expensive flocked Christmas tree. A few days after he and his family had decorated the tree, the branches began to droop. Of course he became rather angry, returned to the store (receipt in hand), and demanded to see the manager.

"My branches are drooping!" exclaimed the customer. The manager responded, "Yes sir, we've had some problems with that load of trees and sent them back. Please feel free to select any other flocked tree you'd like, and we'll even deliver it to you today." The customer thought about it for a moment and said, "Nah, I don't feel like decorating another tree—but I appreciate the offer." Negative Assertion at it's best!

# CHAPTER 7

## ASSERTIVENESS THEORY AND CONFLICT

Each of us is different. However, we all have characteristic tendencies that can place us into certain general categories of behavior.

Although there are specific survey instruments to help reveal your personal characteristics and categorize your behaviorial style, your own observation of others' behavior is often enough to determine their general style.

Following are four general styles of behavior based on the theory of Assertiveness:

1. Aggressive
2. Nonassertive
3. Passive–aggressive
4. Assertive

In considering the profiles of these styles, you can examine their beliefs, actions, verbal cues, and how each style responds to conflict. In the following profiles, consider your boss, a peer, or an employee you may currently be in conflict with. Check off those items you feel describe that person best.

## AGGRESSIVE BEHAVIOR

Aggressive individuals exercise their rights but attempt to take away the rights of others. They operate from a position of dominance, trying to humiliate or put down the other person.

---

### Basic Beliefs

- ☐ "I have rights, but you don't."
- ☐ "My feelings are more important than yours."
- ☐ "I am never wrong."
- ☐ "People should do what I tell them to do."
- ☐ "Don't argue with me."

### Typical Actions

- ☐ Exaggerated show of strength
- ☐ Hands on hips, feet apart, stiff and rigid
- ☐ Abrupt gestures, finger-pointing, fist-pounding
- ☐ Cold, staring eyes; harsh facial expressions
- ☐ Loud voice, demanding, authoritarian

### Verbal Cues

- ☐ "You must . . ." *should ...*
- ☐ "Because I said so . . ."
- ☐ "You dummy . . ."
- ☐ "I'm warning you . . ."
- ☐ "You always [never] . . ."

---

## Handling Conflict

Judging from this profile, it is easy to guess how the Aggressive individual handles differences. Aggressives actually seek conflict, but only with people they know they can dominate. The reason for this is simple—they always go for the Competing or Win/Lose outcome.

Aggressives feel they must win at all costs; therefore, the issue is of little importance—the personal win is what matters. In the process, the Aggressive person will use intimidation, misuse legitimate power, threaten, or personally attack the individual, rather than attempt to find the best outcome for the situation.

## NONASSERTIVE BEHAVIOR

Nonassertives are the opposite of Aggressives. Not only do they not exercise their own rights, they also allow others to take their rights away.

> **Aggressives feel they must win at all costs; therefore, the issue is of little importance—the personal win is what matters.**

### Basic Beliefs

- ☐ "I must be nice."
- ☐ "Don't make waves. If you do, you won't be liked."
- ☐ "Others have rights, but I don't."
- ☐ "I'm not worthy."
- ☐ "If you can't say something nice, don't say anything at all."

### Typical Actions

- ☐ Posturing lacks self-confidence
- ☐ Lots of head nodding (yessing)
- ☐ Eyes averted, downcast
- ☐ Hands fidgety, clammy
- ☐ Voice weak, soft, hesitant

### Verbal Cues

- ☐ "I can't . . ."
- ☐ "I wish . . ."
- ☐ "If only I could . . ."
- ☐ "I'll never be able to . . ."
- ☐ "I probably should . . ."

## Handling Conflict

Nonassertives use Avoidance (Lose/Lose) to deal with conflict whenever they can, and if they can't avoid the issue, they typically manage the situation with Accommodation (Lose/Win). Nonassertives get cold feet when having to face a difficult matter, don't like saying "no" for fear of causing hard feelings, and have a very difficult time making decisions. People using this style may agree externally, while at the same time disagreeing internally. Often, they expect you to guess what they want or what is wrong.

## Unintentional Gunnysacking

Nonassertives unintentionally gunnysack; that is, they gather grievances over a period of time without responding to them when they occur. They figure, "It's no big deal" or "That's OK, I can go along. . . ." But the gunnysack fills, and they become less able to swallow their feelings. At some point, they explode, aggressively dumping the collected grievances on whomever happens to be around. This action is often surprising for two reasons:

1. What caused them to explode didn't seem to be "that big of a deal."
2. Their Aggressive response is completely beyond what you would expect from them.

However unexpected this response may seem, you need to understand that the gunnysacking is still unintentional. Nonassertives intend to please others, so much so, they suffer hurt feelings that may eventually manifest themselves as anger aimed at you.

**Nonassertives intend to please others, so much so, they suffer hurt feelings that may eventually manifest themselves as anger aimed at you.**

## PASSIVE–AGGRESSIVE BEHAVIOR

Passive–Aggressives are initially more difficult to recognize than Aggressives or Nonassertives. Actually this behavior is a combination of the two. At first, this style is nonconfrontive, signaling Nonassertiveness. However, the Passive–Aggressive's ulterior motive is to negatively manipulate the situation in an attempt to ultimately take away the other person's rights, resulting in Aggressive behavior.

### Basic Beliefs

☐ "I'll pay you now, but you'll pay me later."
☐ "Subtle sabotage pays off."
☐ "Better to be cunning than confrontive."
☐ "Never show your cards."
☐ "Don't let them know what you're planning."

### Typical Actions

☐ Flippant, sarcastic style
☐ Air of superiority
☐ Hidden posturing; hands, arms often folded as if concealing
☐ Facial expression does not reveal true feelings
☐ Vocal tone is sometimes "innocent," sometimes "warning"

### Verbal Cues

☐ "Well, if that's the way you want it . . ." (warning tone)
☐ "I told you so . . ." (sing-song effect)
☐ "How could you even think that?" (innocence)
☐ "He/she is obviously mistaken."
☐ "Who . . . me?"

## Handling Conflict

Passive–Aggressives initially choose Avoidance or Accommodation when faced with conflict. However, through negative manipulation, they eventually attempt a Competing (Win/Lose) result. When confronting the Passive–Aggressive, you need to be sure your facts are straight and your issues are in order, because such individuals are very good at manipulating the truth while acting innocent or confused. Additionally, Passive–Aggressives will often *suggest* that the fault lies with someone else they had probably warned you about earlier.

## Intentional Gunnysacking

Passive–Aggressives, like Nonassertives, also gunnysack—but with a difference. They do it intentionally. Although they initially Accommodate (passive), they also collect any and all items that could be used against someone at a later date. It is at this point that the aggressive side surfaces, resulting in a "gotcha!" outcome.

> **Passive–Aggressives are also referred to as "snipers," because of their tendency to blindside about people whenever possible.**

Passive–Aggressives are also referred to as "snipers," because of their tendency to blindside other people whenever possible.

# ASSERTIVE BEHAVIOR

Assertive individuals exercise their rights and encourage others to do the same. Of the four behaviors in Assertiveness theory, this style is the most well balanced. Assertives are honest, and show consideration for the feelings and opinions of others.

## Handling Conflict

Assertive individuals handle conflict very well, often attempting Collaboration (Win/Win). Of course, this is the

## Basic Beliefs

- ☐ "I have rights and so do others."
- ☐ "People deserve my respect."
- ☐ "I may not always win, but I can always manage the situation."
- ☐ "It's best to deal with issues when they occur."
- ☐ "Mistakes can be corrected."

## Typical Actions

- ☐ General assured manner
- ☐ Communicates caring and strength
- ☐ Uses "I" rather than "you" messages
- ☐ Sincere facial expressions, direct eye contact
- ☐ Voice is firm, well modulated, nonthreatening

## Verbal Cues

- ☐ "What are our options?"
- ☐ "You're right, it's my mistake."
- ☐ "What will you do to . . . ?"
- ☐ "I choose to . . ."
- ☐ "What are the real issues here?"

most difficult result to achieve, so the assertive person is prepared for Compromise (Win/Lose–Win/Lose) when necessary. Additionally, this behavioral style is also capable of Accommodation (Lose/Win) when the issue's relative importance to the other party can be determined. Last in their choice would be either Avoidance or Competing, although they are aware that when all else fails, the choices are limited.

In short, Assertives choose the appropriate conflict management method according to the person and situation.

Based on your checkmarks in each profile, which behavioral category does the person you're in conflict with
resemble the most?

Which profile do *you* resemble the most?

# CHAPTER 8

## MATCHING BEHAVIORAL STYLES TO MANAGE DIFFERENCES

After you identify someone's particular style of behavior—Aggressive, Nonassertive, Passive–Aggressive, or Assertive—you are in a better position to resolve or at least manage differences with this person because you can often predict his or her reactions in conflicting situations.

We now consider a summary profile of the four behavioral styles and the preferred matching behaviors to best respond to each one.

### SUMMARY PROFILE: AGGRESSIVES

| | |
|---|---|
| *Definition:* | Exercises own rights; attempts to take away rights of others |
| *Behavior:* | Intimidates, demands, attempts to conquer at all costs |
| *Conflict Management Method:* | Competing |
| *Preferred Matching Behaviors:* | Nonassertiveness, assertiveness, aggressiveness |

When attempting to handle the Aggressive, we need to consider our current relationship and possible future consequences before choosing the preferred matching behavior.

55

## Responding Nonassertively

If you choose to respond nonassertively, you take the path of least risk and least resistance. This works very well when dealing with the Aggressive individual because you are giving this person exactly what he or she wants—a win at the expense of your loss. Although this might sound unreasonable to many people, it happens all the time in the workplace.

The big question is the cost. You should consider a few questions before deciding whether or not to choose the nonassertive response.

- Is it worth it, in this situation, to give in?
- Will it become the norm whenever you deal with this individual?
- Are you backing off simply because you never choose to confront?
- Will you fall prey to this individual in the future?

It is important for you to realize that responding nonassertively should actually be an assertive choice for justifiable reasons, and not simply a continuance of typical nonassertive behavior.

## Responding Assertively

A second matching behavior when dealing with the Aggressive individual is the assertive response. This involves a higher degree of risk because you prevent the other person from taking away your personal rights. In effect, you are standing up for yourself. There are two possible results to this position:

1. The Aggressive person will compete even harder in an attempt to overcome you.
2. The Aggressive person will back off, realizing that a limit has been reached and you can't be pushed around further. After this limit is established, it is

much easier to focus on the issues rather than on who has the stronger personality.

## Responding Aggressively

**Sometimes, the only way to deal with Aggressives is to give them a taste of their own medicine.**

Sometimes, the only way to deal with Aggressives is to give them a taste of their own medicine. This is exactly what you do when you choose an aggressive response. However, here you incur the highest degree of risk. If the other person doesn't back down, the situation will surely intensify. On the other hand, sometimes when aggressive behavior is met with aggressive behavior, the end result is not only backing down, but also an establishment of respect. The Aggressive realizes that not only can your rights not be invaded, but aggressive behavior will be met head on with aggressive behavior.

## SUMMARY PROFILE: NONASSERTIVES

| | |
|---|---|
| *Definition:* | Does not exercise personal rights; allows others to take them away |
| *Behavior:* | Continually gives in, avoids conflict, tries to please everyone, puts off decisions |
| *Conflict Management Method:* | Avoidance, Accommodation |
| *Preferred Matching Behavior:* | Assertiveness |

When responding to Nonassertives, the most appropriate behavioral response is Assertive. Because Assertives are sensitive to the needs of others, they are capable of helping the Nonassertive to exercise his or her rights.

Assertives can also help in encouraging the decision-making process. For example, you can ask the Nonassertive how a particular situation should be handled. Even though the answer may not be your personal choice, it may still be a valid approach. Through Accommodation, you can then encourage the Nonassertive to follow through with the suggested approach, thus increasing his or her self-confidence.

Of course, you can intimidate Nonassertives through aggressiveness or manipulate them through passive–aggressiveness, but your intention should be focused on building a healthy working relationship rather than taking advantage of their behavioral style.

## SUMMARY PROFILE: PASSIVE– AGGRESSIVES

| | |
|---|---|
| *Definition:* | Initially passive; eventually attempts to take away the rights of others |
| *Behavior:* | Avoids direct confrontation, claims innocence, attempts to twist things around, is sneaky |
| *Conflict Management Method:* | Accommodation, Competition |
| *Preferred Matching Response:* | Assertiveness |

Passive–Aggressives are perhaps the most difficult type to handle. Because they are manipulative, it's difficult to clearly recognize exactly what they're up to at any given time. An assertive response gives us the best opportunity to effectively handle this behavior.

The temptation when dealing with the Passive–Aggressive is to become either aggressive or to also respond in passive–aggressive style. Neither of these responses, however, will get you very far. If you respond aggressively, you run the risk of "losing it," which is exactly what the Passive–

Aggressive wants. Yelling, finger pointing, and fist pounding only gives such an individual the satisfaction that he or she has been able to "press your buttons," causing you to become upset and lose control while they remain calm. It's another form of "gotcha!"

If you try to respond with passive–aggressive behavior, you walk into their ballpark where they wrote the rules, and they won't give you a copy. In addition, they're likely to change the rulebook at any time—but, of course, you won't know it.

**Because the Passive–Aggressive is a game player, and games absorb an enormous amount of productive time, the best approach is the assertive response.**

Because the Passive–Aggressive is a game player, and games absorb an enormous amount of productive time, the best approach is the assertive response. By getting your facts straight beforehand and resisting any attempt to twist things around or claim innocence or blame someone else, you can more effectively manage them and focus on the issues. You need to be very specific when discussing incidents and also with your expectations of their behavior.

## SUMMARY PROFILE: ASSERTIVES

| | |
|---|---|
| *Definition:* | Exercises own rights; encourages others to do the same |
| *Behavior:* | Communicates caring and strength: listens well; general assured manner |
| *Conflict Management Method:* | Collaboration; uses other methods when the situation warrants |
| *Preferred Matching Behavior:* | Assertiveness |

Assertives are the easiest types of individuals to respond to. Because they are concerned with both production and people, working with them is a pleasure. Communications are open. If you disagree, you can say so. If you need to constructively criticize, you can do that too. With the Assertive, you can resolve conflicts through Collaboration. When both parties are mutually assertive, the focus is on issues, rather than personalities.

Responding to Assertives by being assertive gives you the opportunity to learn more about both yourself and them while accomplishing much more than you could with any of the other styles.

It's easy to see that responding assertively is the key in dealing with all four of the behavioral styles. Aggressiveness, nonassertiveness, and passive–aggressiveness all have hidden agendas, whether intentioned or not. Your focus needs to be on the management of issues and on resolution of differences rather than on controlling, always giving in to, or manipulating others. By choosing assertiveness as a response, you will be able to look at issues objectively, consider the behavioral style of the individual(s) involved, and respond appropriately.

# CHAPTER 9

## MANAGING CONFLICT AMONG BOSSES, PEERS, AND EMPLOYEES

Although conflict occurs at all levels of the organization, we personally face differences at three levels: bosses, peers, and, if we supervise, employees. As mentioned earlier, the real issue is not so much that conflict occurs, but rather how you handle it when it does.

The psychodynamics and possible consequences are different with each level; therefore, you need to consider each level separately. However, whatever the level, there are four questions you need to consider in determining your approach to the person with whom you have a conflict.

1. What is the person's behavioral style when conflict occurs?
2. What is the person's usual method of handling conflict?
3. What might he or she value in this situation?
4. What should your approach be?

In addition to considering how to manage conflict with someone, you should also examine certain measures you can take to work more effectively with others, whatever their level may be.

61

**Bosses: Some are great, most are OK, but a few are really miserable.**

# MANAGING CONFLICT WITH BOSSES

Bosses: Some are great, most are OK, and a few are really miserable. But great, OK, or miserable, the boss is still the boss, and it's to your advantage to accept that fact and work toward resolving conflict when it occurs, or toward preventing it from happening in the first place.

When you are in conflict with those above you in the organization, you are at the highest level of risk. You are also somewhat limited in the approaches that can be taken. For example, it wouldn't normally be considered wise to attempt the Competing approach with an Aggressive boss. Sometimes, even the possibility of Compromise may be out of the question. But although there is the possibility for greater consequences with these approaches, you also have the possibility of success, depending on how you approach the individual. Consider the following case study:

**Case Study:** Ed B. manages a department of thirteen professional staff members. You have worked for him for two years. He has a reputation for being loud, rude, and hard-nosed with most of his employees—you included. In past conflicts, you've tried to argue your point, but to no avail. Because of these disagreements, your relationship seems to have deteriorated. You want to salvage the situation, but you're not the nonassertive type. On the other hand, Ed B. loves to give orders without giving reasons.

    1. What is Ed B.'s probable behavioral style when in conflict?

        _____

    2. What is his probable method of handling conflict?

        _____

    3. What might he value in this situation?

        _____

4. What would a low-risk approach be? What would be the probable results?

_____

_____

_____

5. What would a high-risk approach be? What would be the probable results?

_____

_____

_____

The next study is the real thing. Choose someone above you in your organization with whom you have experienced conflict.

Name: _____

1. What is his/her usual behavioral style when in conflict?

_____

2. What is his/her usual method of handling conflict?

_____

3. What does he/she value when involved in conflict?

_____

4. What would a low-risk approach be? What would be the probable results?

_____

_____

_____

5. What would a high-risk approach be? What would the probable results be?

_____

_____

_____

6. Do your answers differ from the way you've handled conflicting situations with this person in the past? If so, what will your approach be now?

_____

_____

_____

## Working More Effectively With Bosses

As mentioned earlier, you can often prevent conflicts from happening in the first place. It may mean adjustments on your part, but often the cost is small when compared to the potential conflict.

**A major help in working more effectively with bosses is to adapt your workplace values to theirs where you can.**

We tend to get along better with people who have values similar to our own. A major help in working more effectively with bosses is to adapt your *workplace* values to theirs where you can. This doesn't mean changing your life-style, but it does imply a willingness to make certain changes and perhaps a few concessions . . . in other words, a willingness to use a combination of Compromise and Accommodation to help build the relationship.

Consider the following questions for working better with your boss.

### Questions for Working More Effectively With Your Boss

1. When does your boss arrive? Leave?

_____

2. Does your boss take long or short lunches, frequent or few breaks?

_____

3.  How neat is your boss's workplace?

_____

4.  What time of the day is your boss most receptive to you?

_____

5.  Does your boss prefer written or verbal reports? Concise or detailed?

_____

6.  Does your boss welcome new ideas or resist them?

_____

7.  What is your boss's behavioral style?

_____

8.  How could you change your style accordingly?

_____

When answering these questions you may discover value differences between yourself and your boss. The point is: Where can you compromise? Where can you accommodate? What is it worth to you? Sometimes, you might think it would be much easier just to be left alone so you could do your job. But your relationship with your boss (whether you agree or not) always plays a critical role in your success or failure in the workplace.

## MANAGING CONFLICT WITH PEERS

Managing conflict with peers doesn't carry the same potential risk encountered when dealing with bosses. With peers, there is more flexibility to explore potential approaches and possible results for managing differences. For example, with equals, it might be appropriate to attempt competing if the situation warranted, or perhaps you could insist on at least resolving the issue through compromise.

However, even though you may have more flexibility when dealing with peers, it is still important to be able to work well with them. This includes not only colleagues in your department but other departments as well. How you perform your job is important, but how you deal with others is just as important. Consider the following case study:

**How you perform your job is important, but how you deal with others is just as important.**

**Case Study.** Grace S. is a newly hired colleague in your department. You both were assigned to an interdepartmental team about six weeks ago. Initially, things seemed to be going well. But two members of the team recently approached you indicating Grace's concern about some negative comments she said you made regarding the team's direction. The truth is you like the direction the team is moving in, have never made any negative comments, and enjoy being a member of this group effort. You later approached Grace about this, and she appeared offended that you could even think such a thing and denied saying anything to anybody. Then yesterday, your boss called you in to let you know he had heard from a confidential source that the team was concerned about your behavior.

1. What is Grace S.'s probable behavioral style?

   _____

2. What is her probable method of handling conflict?

   _____

3. What might she value in this situation?

   _____

4. What would a low-risk approach be? What would be the probable results?

   _____

   _____

   _____

5. What would a high-risk approach be? What would be the probable results?

_____

_____

_____

Again, the real thing. Choose a colleague with whom you have experienced conflict

Name: _____

1. What is his/her usual behavioral style?

_____

2. What is his/her usual method of handling conflict?

_____

3. What might he/she value when involved in conflict?

_____

4. What would a low-risk approach be? What would be the probable results?

_____

_____

_____

5. What would a high-risk approach be? What would be the probable results?

_____

_____

_____

6. Do your answers differ from the way you've handled conflicting situations with this person in the past? If so, what will your approach be now?

_____

_____

_____

## Working More Effectively With Peers

With so much emphasis on team building and team membership, the ability to work well with your peers is an important characteristic in the workplace. Often, it is a major factor in determining who is chosen for special projects—as team leaders or even for promotion.

Following are some questions for you to consider when attempting to work more effectively with peers.

### Questions for Working More Effectively With Peers

1. Do you both respect and understand each other's roles? Briefly describe them.

   _____

   _____

2. Do you understand each other's tasks? Briefly list them.

   _____

   _____

   _____

3. Are there agreed-to time frames you are both meeting?

   _____

4. Are each of you willing to confront and deal with differences?

   _____

5. How well do both of you handle Compromise?

_____

_____

If you are currently in conflict with a peer, using the answers to these questions as a base for managing the differences will help.

Of course, somebody's got to go first—and you're the one reading this book.

## Managing Conflict With Employees

When you begin managing others, you step into a new level of awareness. Although you gain the power of reward and punishment, you also become much more accountable for your actions. Fairness becomes a critical factor.

For example, although you may not personally like a particular employee, you do not necessarily have the right to act out those feelings. As a manager or supervisor, you are obligated to be fair, regardless of your personal feelings. You are also obligated to develop your employees to the highest possible level, and to appraise their performance and behavior as objectively as you can.

When you are having differences with an employee, you need to be aware of two possibly conflicting issues: On the one hand you have complete flexibility of choosing any of the five methods of conflict resolution; on the other hand, you need to be careful not to *misuse* certain methods such as Competing. Even though you have the power to force the Win/Lose outcome, you need to give fair consideration when choosing your approach to the situation. Consider the following case study:

**Case Study:** You hired Lucille P. approximately a year ago. She is a very pleasant employee, but has a difficult time accepting any kind of criticism. Her work performance fluctuates between needing improvement and acceptable. Each time you've tried to give her constructive criticism, she's become emotional and then withdrawn; so you've recently avoided discussing her job performance.

Although you don't want to cause further conflict with her, you really believe Lucille P. can become a valued employee. In addition, you have to give her annual performance review in two weeks.

1. What is Lucille P.'s probable behavioral style?

   _____

2. What is her probable method of handling conflict?

   _____

3. What might she value in this situation?

   _____

4. What would a low-risk approach to her performance review be? What would be the probable results?

   _____

   _____

   _____

5. What would a high-risk approach be? What would be the probable results?

   _____

   _____

   _____

The final real thing. Choose an employee with whom you are currently experiencing conflict.

Name: _____

1. What is his/her usual behavioral style?

   _____

2. What is his/her usual method of handling conflict?

   _____

3. What does he/she value when involved in conflict?

   _____

4. What would a low-risk approach be? What would be the probable results?

   _____

   _____

   _____

5. What would a high-risk approach be? What would be the probable results?

   _____

   _____

   _____

6. Do your answers differ from the way you've handled conflicting situations with this person in the past? If so, what will your approach be now?

   _____

   _____

   _____

**The key factor when you manage others is that you are the controlling influence.**

## Working More Effectively With Employees

As with bosses and peers, there are measures you can take to prevent many conflicts from occuring. The key factor when you manage others is that you are the controlling influence. You set the atmosphere for those you manage.

Consider using the following questions when working with employees.

## Questions for Working More Effectively With Employees

1. When do you make yourself available to your employees?

   _____

2. Do you get back to them when you say you will?

   _____

3. What active listening skills do you use? Which skills do you still need to develop?

   _____

   _____

4. Do you criticize constructively or destructively?

   _____

5. What methods do you use to resolve differences with employees?

   _____

   _____

6. What do you do to help them develop additional skills?

   _____

   _____

7. What do you do to encourage them to take on more challenging tasks?

   _____

   _____

8. What do you know about their personal lives?

   _____

The more questions you are able to answer positively, the greater the possibility you are establishing a positive atmosphere, and the lesser is the probability of unnecessary conflict. Not only can you provide the opportunity for growth and success for them and you, you can also help to prevent your company from the possibility of unnecessary grievances or other legal problems.

In short, if the atmosphere is positive, conflicts will be minimized. And if the atmosphere is negative, you should not only expect the worst, you should also accept the responsibility for having created it through poor management.

However, it's never too late for positive change.

# CHAPTER 10

## A WORD ABOUT TEAM BUILDING AND CONFLICT

Team building. It's an explosion. Everyone's doing it, or will be, and there's no end in sight. But there's a problem. While companies are insisting, "We're a team! We're a team!" many aren't providing the orientation as to what it really means, and a lot of "teams" aren't doing so well.

**Questions About Your Team**

1. What role are you currently in: member? leader?

   _____

2. What tasks are you personally responsible for?

   _____

   _____

3. Are you personally involved in a conflict with another team member? Considering the information in this book, what could you do to manage the situation?

   _____

   _____

4. What other conflicts exist within the team?

   _____

   _____

5. What needs to be done?

_____

_____

6. Are there any members who don't want to "play"?
   Describe.

_____

_____

7. What do you think the team should do?

_____

_____

8. How is the leadership? If strong, why? If weak, what
   could be done?

_____

_____

**Because managing conflict is a necessary part of high-performance team building, you need to consider the relationship between team building and conflict.**

Team building isn't a new idea, but it is a concept reborn, and conflict is certainly a part of it. As in any relationship, differences will occur in teams, perhaps even more, because there are usually more than two people involved.

## THE BASICS OF TEAM BUILDING AND CONFLICT

Too often, when differences occur in team meetings, they are simply smoothed over by the leader or other members. Of course, in these cases the conflict doesn't dissipate; it just simmers until a later date. The only thing accomplished is the gradual building up of resentment between team members. Because managing conflict is a necessary part of high-performance team building, you need to consider the relationship between team building and conflict.

## Decision Making: Voting vs. Consensus

When teams are allowed to make their own decisions, there are two possibilities: voting or consensus.

1. *Voting.* Although voting is quicker, it can help promote division within the team. When there is a vote on decisions, there are winners and losers. In teams, the idea is for everyone to agree on the decision.

2. *Consensus.* Reaching consensus is more difficult than voting, but it is the preferred approach to team-building decisions. It does, of course, take longer, and differences will occur in the process. But in the end, everyone supports the final decision.

## Membership

Being a member of a team is not easy for a lot of us, especially if we're accustomed to making decisions on our own. When you become a team player, you enter into an interdependent relationship. You may even feel you're giving up your individuality. In one sense you are, but in another sense you are making an individual contribution to a group effort that usually produces a greater end result than you could have achieved on your own.

Consider the following elements of team membership dynamics.

1. *Participation.* As a team member, you are expected to participate in a balanced manner; that is, to not be dominant or withdrawn, and at the same time help others to maintain their own balance.

2. *Selling.* You probably feel your ideas are great. Sometimes they are. Your responsibility as a team member is to prepare ahead of time, whenever possible, and to present your ideas in a logical way to show the team "What's In It For Them (WIIFT)?" You also need to be able to defend your position with logic rather than emotion. Emotional defenses usually lead to conflict between personalities rather than focusing on the issues.

3. *Relinquishing.* This is the big one. What if you sell to the best of your ability, but the team won't buy? Some team members temporarily withdraw. Some don't want to play anymore . . . ever. This is the point where the rest of the team discovers what kind of team player you really are. Your responsibility at this point is to relinquish your position even though you really believe yours is the better idea. Not only do you need to give it up, you must also be willing to support and even defend the team's direction in favor of your own. It's not easy, but as a team player it's the whole that counts, not an individual part.

4. *Evaluating.* After a team project is completed, each member is responsible for participating in a group evaluation. What worked? What could have been done better? How could it be done differently next time? *However,* under no circumstances are the words, "I told you so . . ." ever to cross any member's lips in the evaluation process.

5. *Relationship.* As a team member, you are responsible for your relationship with other team members. If there is a personal conflict, it is up to you to do what you can to resolve a conflict. Personal conflicts in team efforts fracture and sometimes totally prevent task accomplishment.

6. *Task Accomplishment.* When acting as a team member, it is critical that you are clear on your task responsibility. This includes what you have to do, when it has to be done by, and any steps in between. In an interdependent relationship, one member's failure can trigger the delay of others' efforts and affect the outcome of the entire team. Being a good team player isn't easy. Bringing excess baggage, using hidden agendas, or protecting authorship of personal ideas all serve to prevent the overall direction. You can better serve yourself and the other members if you focus on what's best for the team rather than yourself.

> **In an interdependent relationship, one member's failure can trigger the delay of others' efforts and affect the outcome of the entire team.**

## Leadership

Another area where companies have failed to provide good orientation regarding team building is in leadership. Sometimes groups are simply told, "Go be a team, make consensus decisions, and, by the way, everybody's equal." Well, everyone may be equal, but newly formed teams need leaders, and even sophisticated teams need facilitators to keep things moving.

Leaders can be appointed or elected, but in the beginning *someone* must be in control. Leadership has certain responsibilities that are different from those of membership. Consider the following list of leadership requirements.

1. *Managing Conflict.* If team members fail to resolve issues themselves, it is the leader's responsibility to surface the issues so they can be discussed, examined, and concluded. Sometimes this is best done privately, but sometimes it may be better to involve the team as a whole.

2. *Controlling Uncooperative Members.* If there is an individual on the team who is aggressive in team interaction, it may be up to the team leader to counsel with the individual regarding his or her behavior. In severe situations, this may even include asking the member to leave the team. Anyone can be replaced, and it's unfair for the team to have to be held back because of one individual.

3. *Drawing Out Nonassertives.* Some team members may have very good ideas but have difficulty speaking out in a group. Here the team leader has two issues to deal with: getting the member's ideas outside the team setting and encouraging the individual to be more assertive in his or her interaction within the team setting.

4. *Conducting Productive Meetings.* There are two types of meetings: productive and ridiculous. The only one worth mentioning is productive.

Following are some hints for having productive meetings.

- Have an agenda in advance, with time limits for each item.
- Start on time (a minor miracle).
- Stay on track.
- End with everyone knowing their specific assignments and timetables.

- End on time (a historical event).
- Send minutes to team members within two days following each meeting.

5. *Remaining Objective.* Team leaders, although also team members, must be objective enough to manage both tasks and relationships. They need to be involved as a functioning member and also be able to extricate themselves so they can observe both group dynamics and task progress.

Although team membership is not an easy job, team leadership is even more complex. Leading a team requires an individual who wants the position, is capable of directing task accomplishment, and has an understanding of the dynamics involved in a group effort.

Team building requires the efforts of everyone involved. Companies need to be willing to provide the necessary training to get their teams off to a good start. Without it an organization will flounder in conflict, unresolved differences, and failed tasks. But if the proper orientation is provided, a lot can be accomplished.

# NOTES

# NOTES

# NOTES